THIS OCTOPUS BELONGS TO

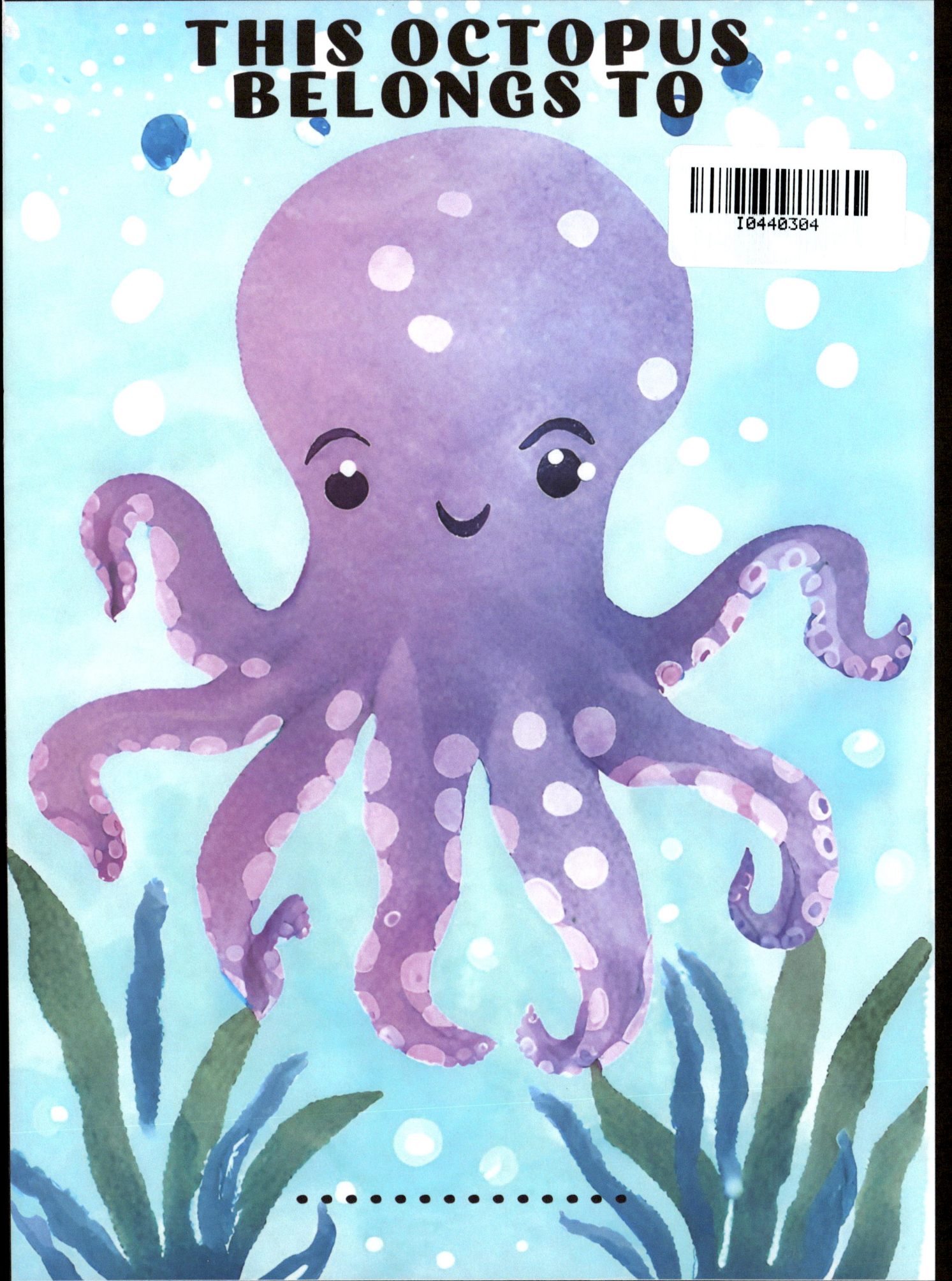

· · · · · · · · · · · · · · · · ·

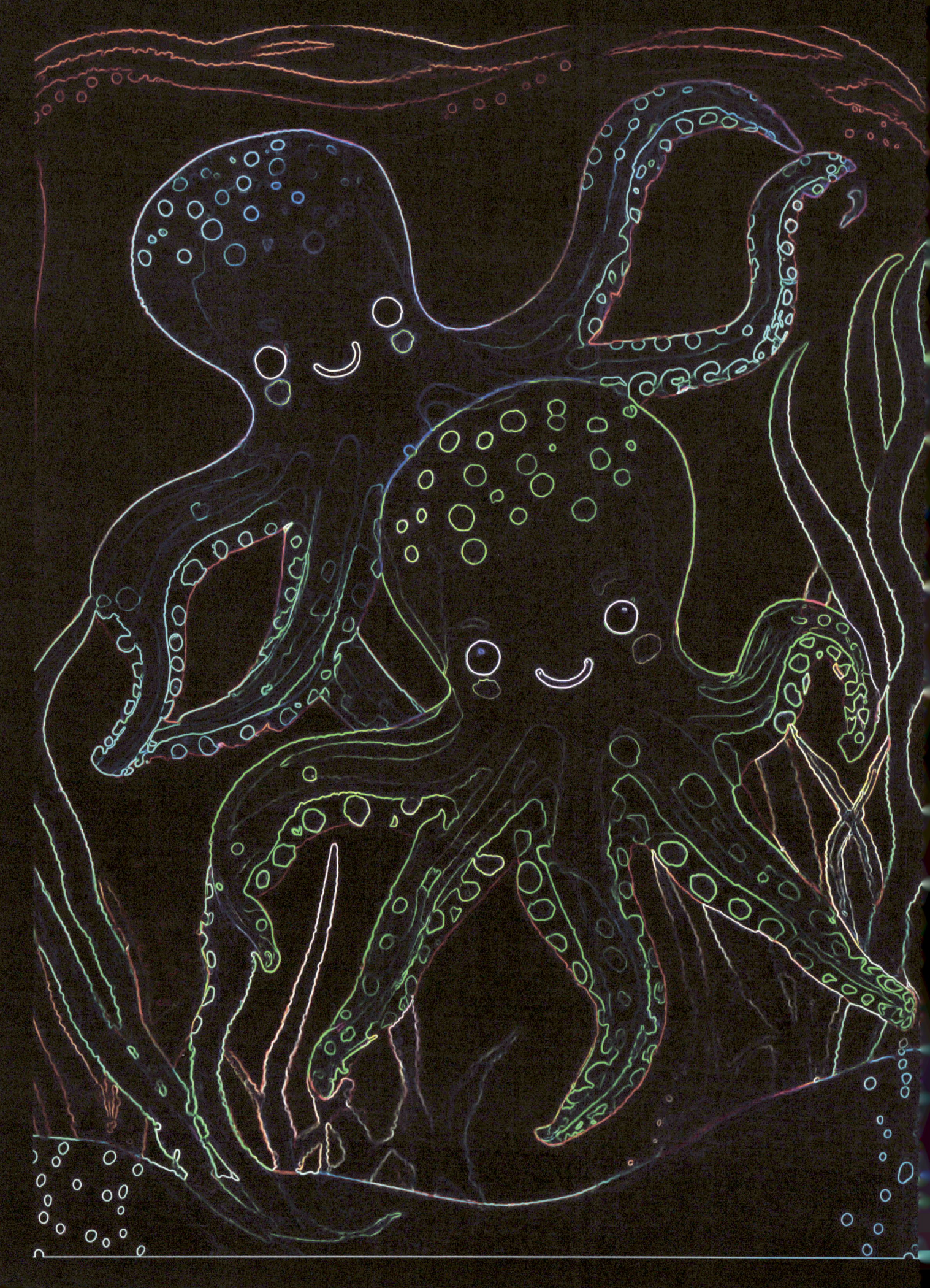

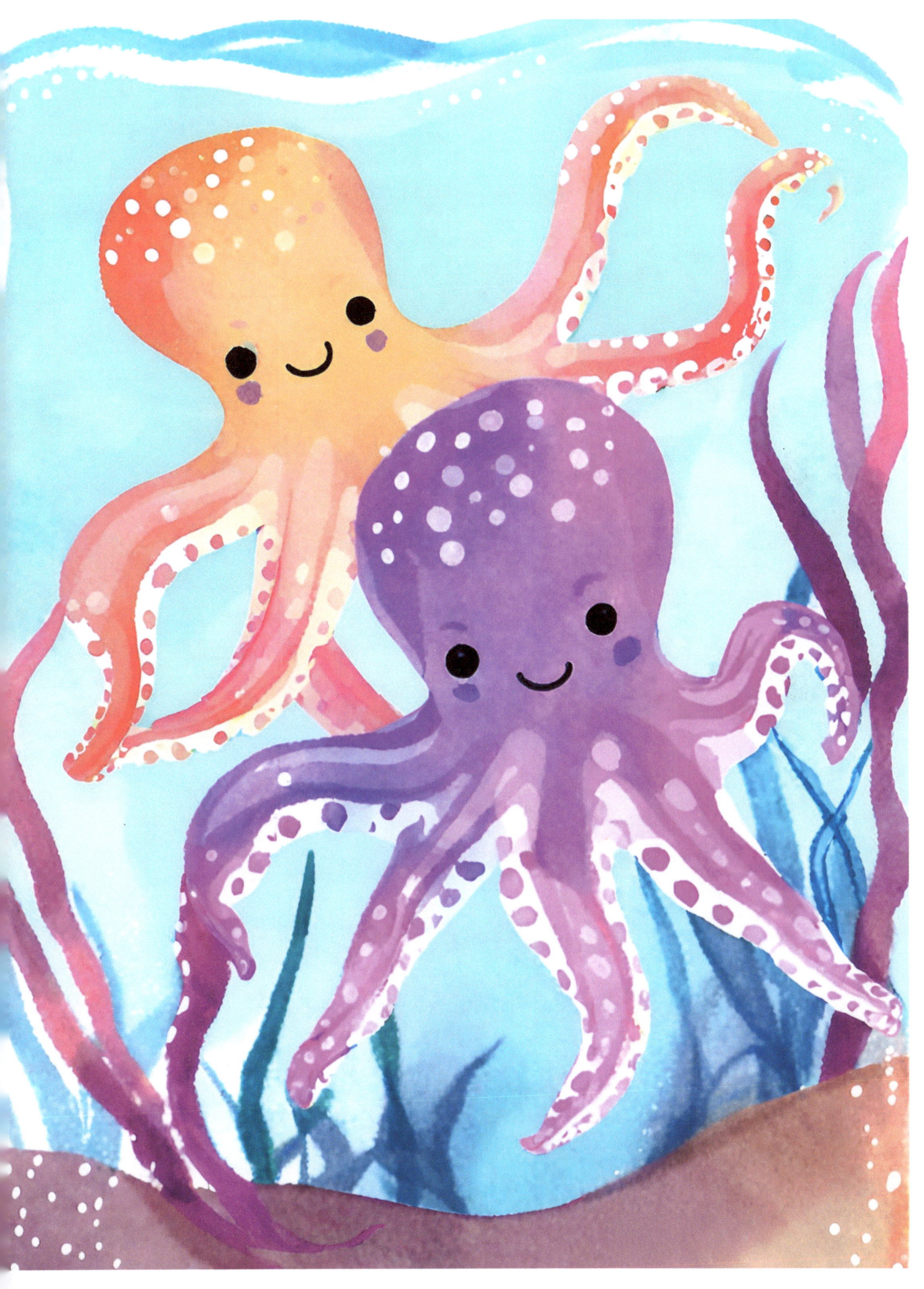

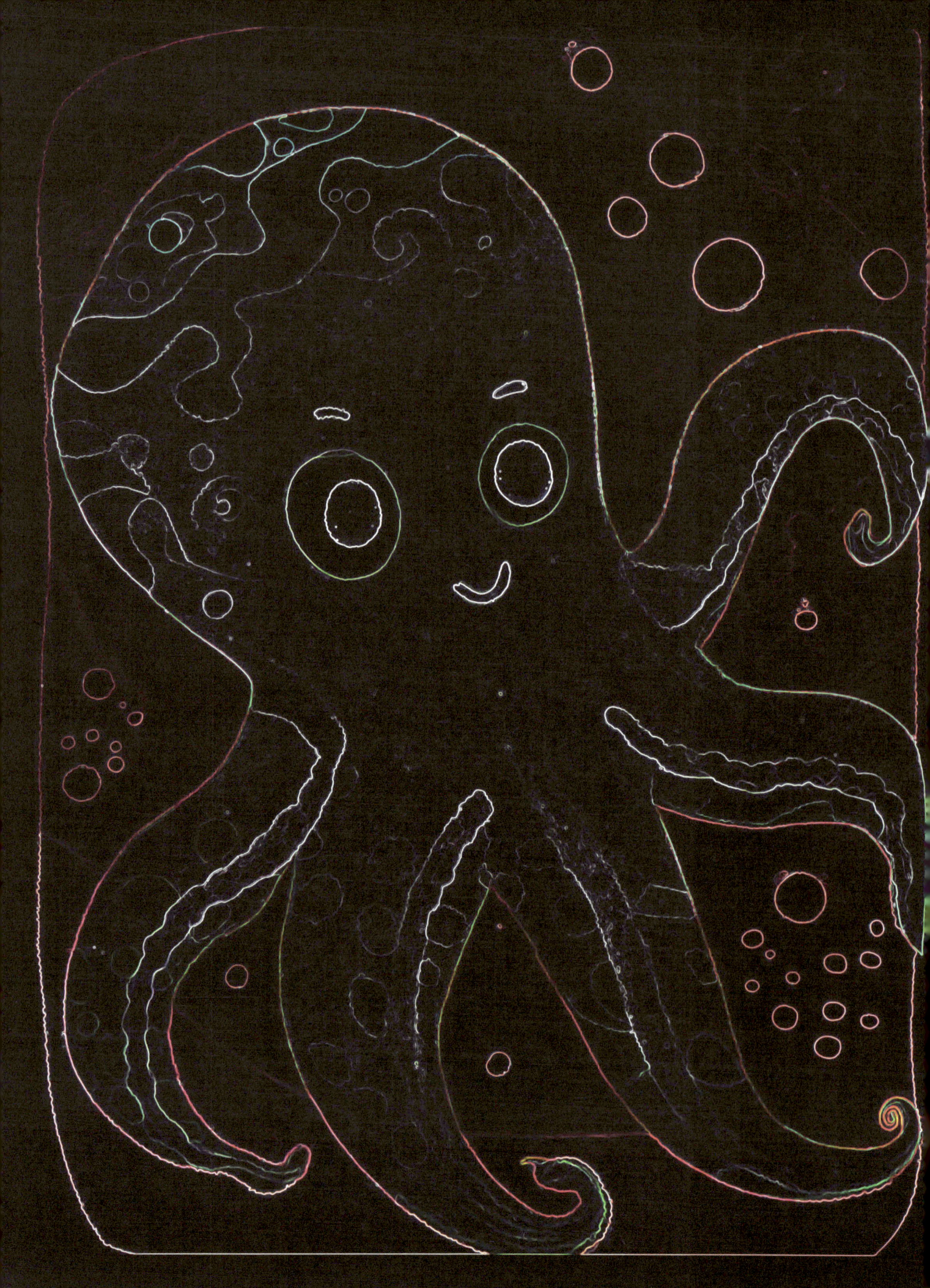

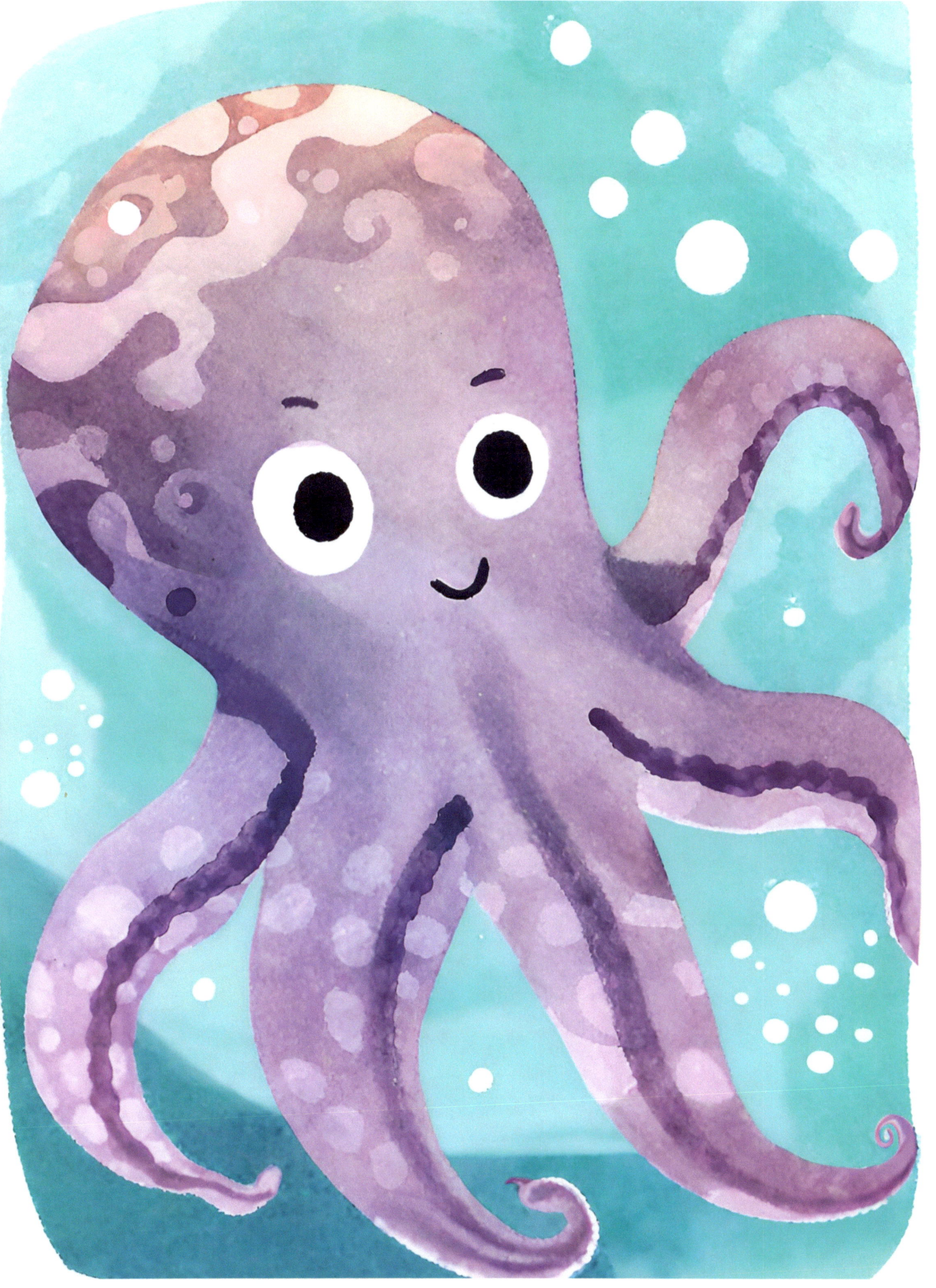

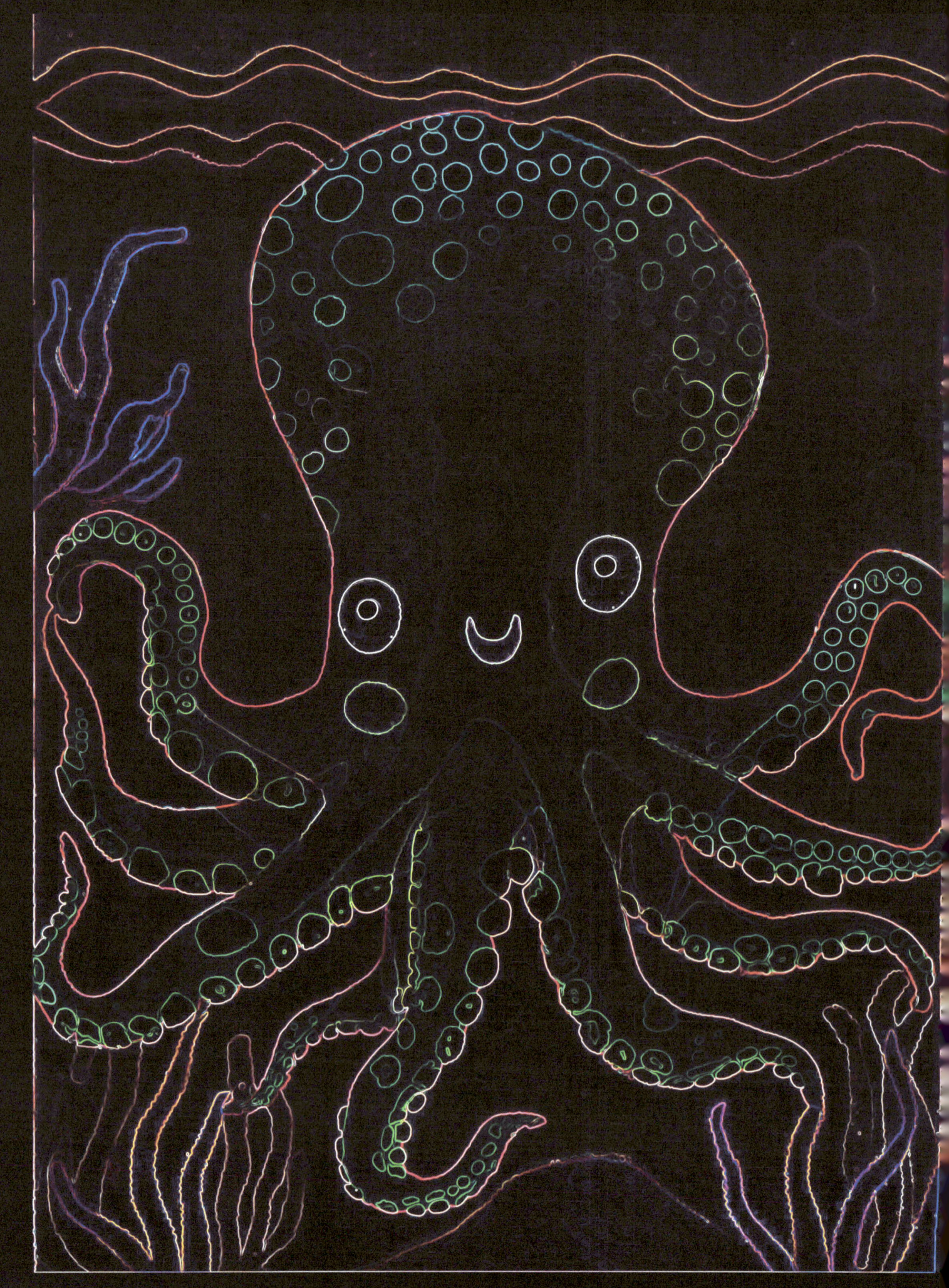

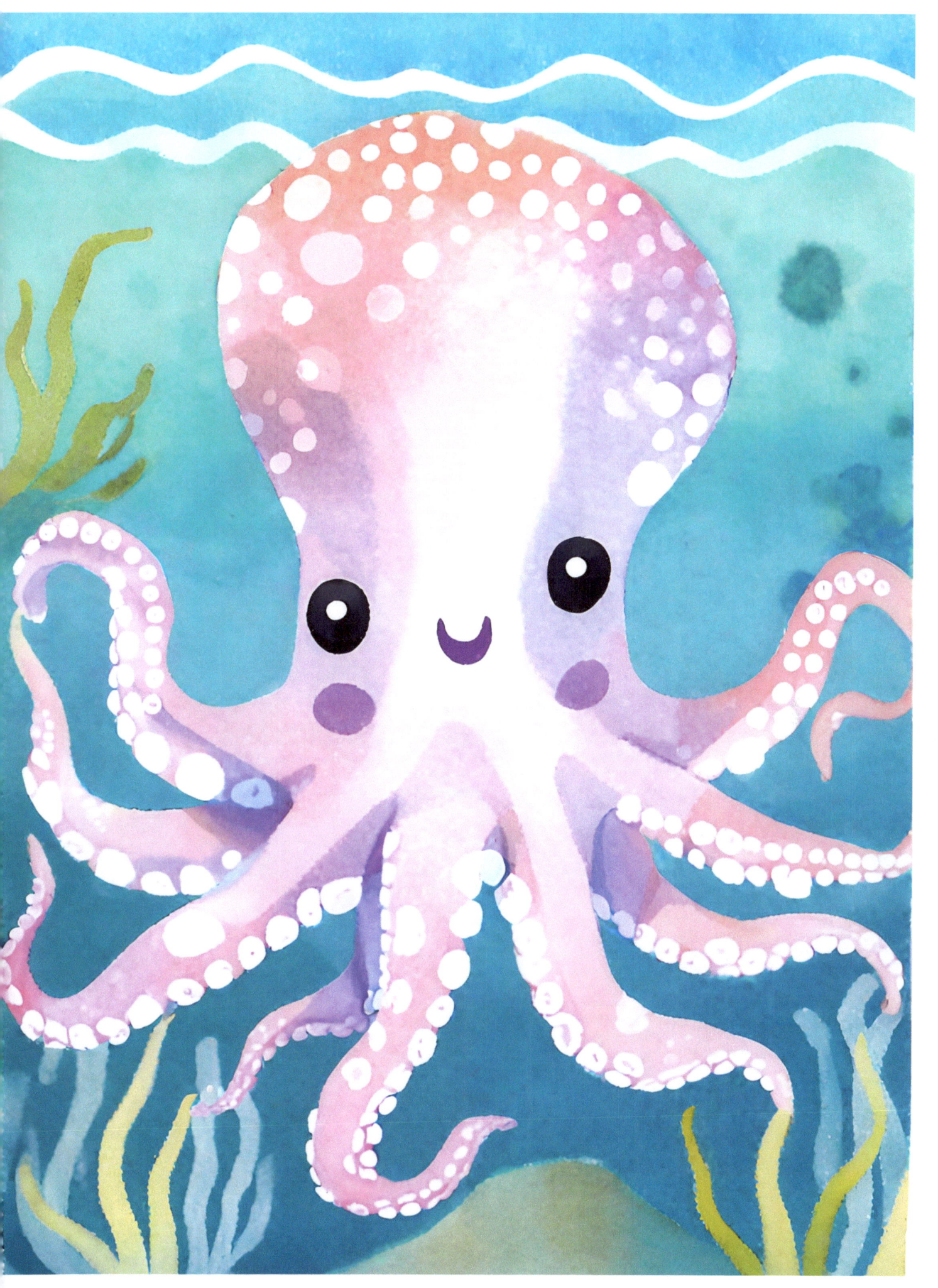

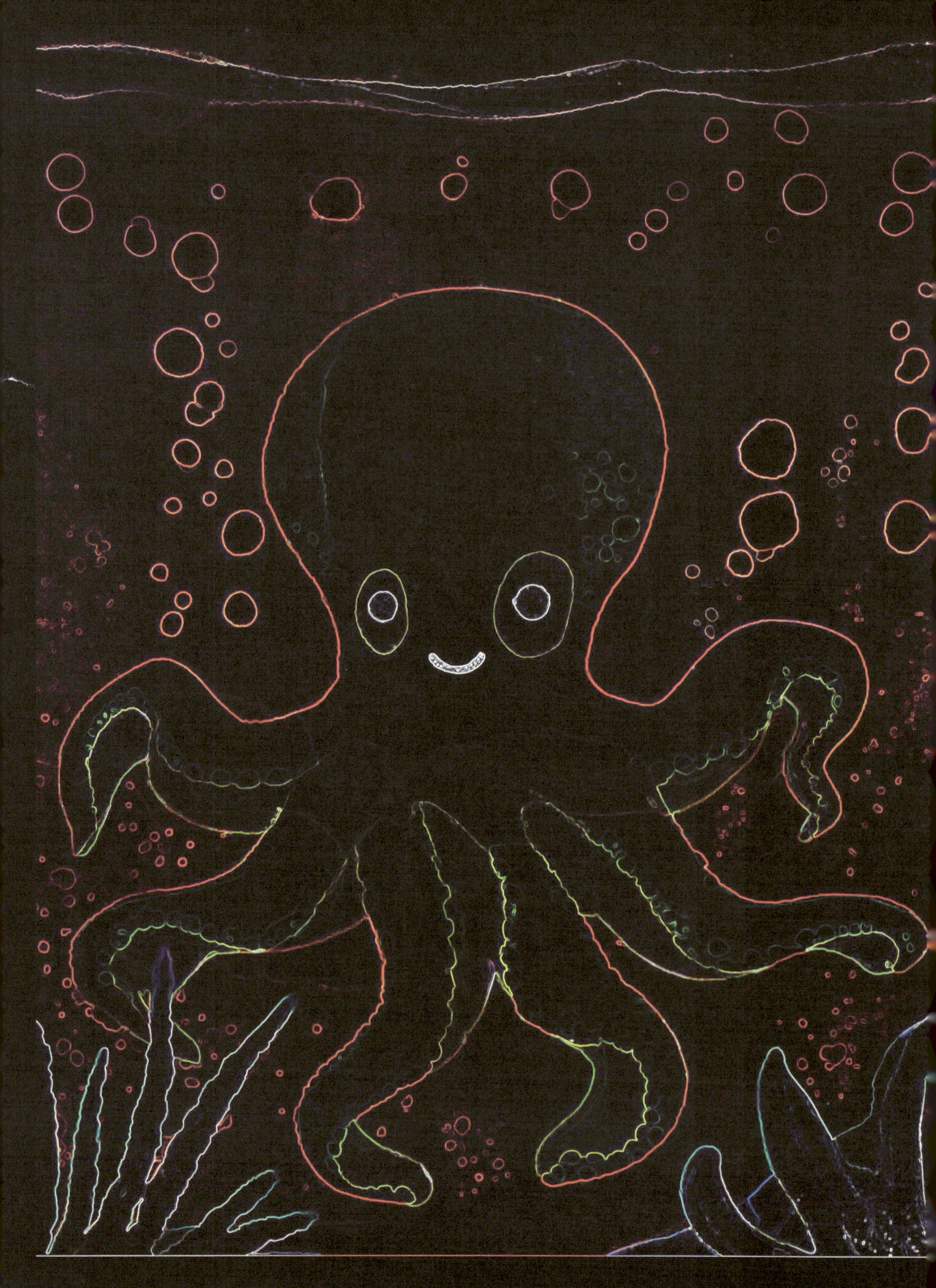

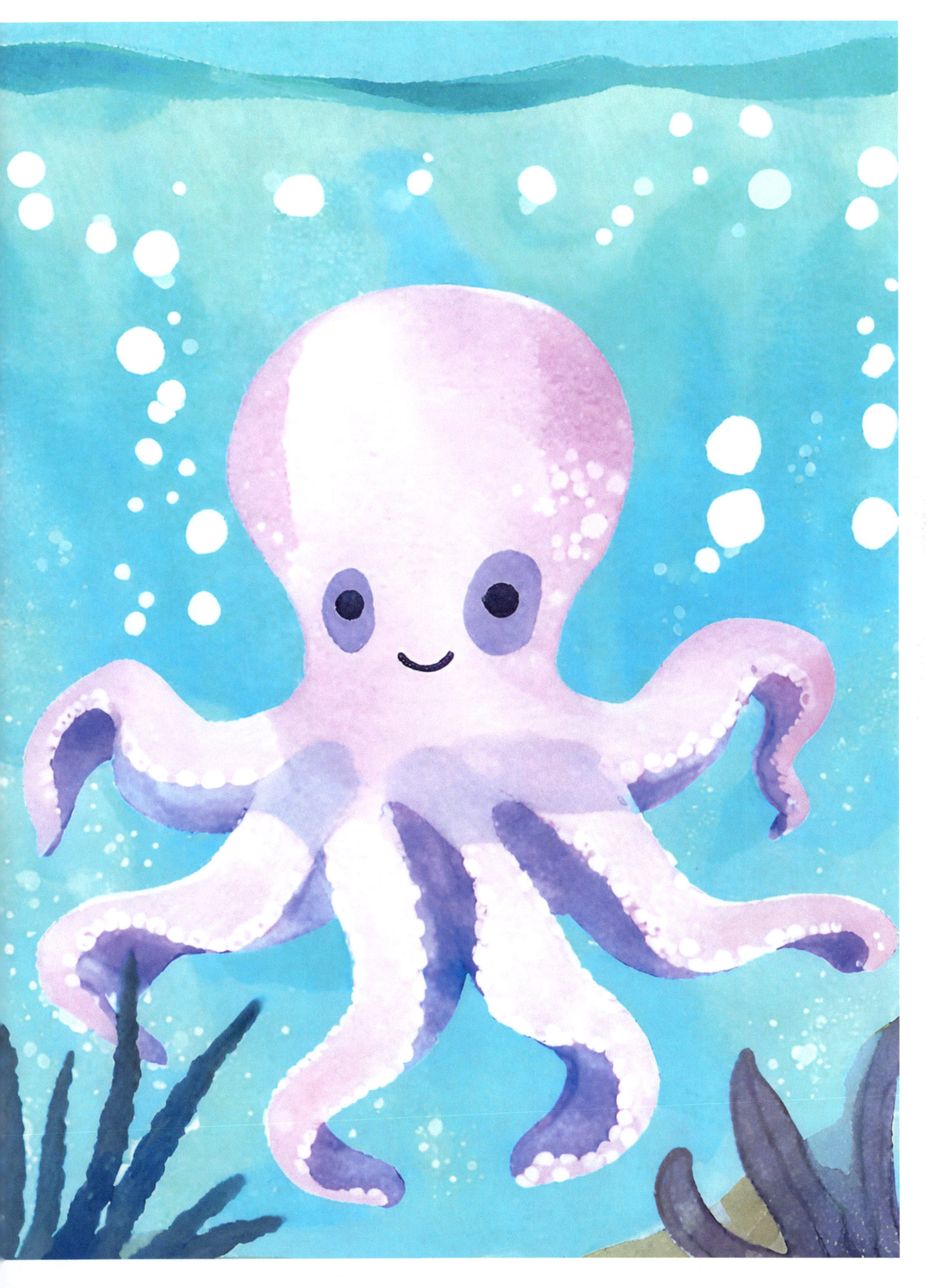

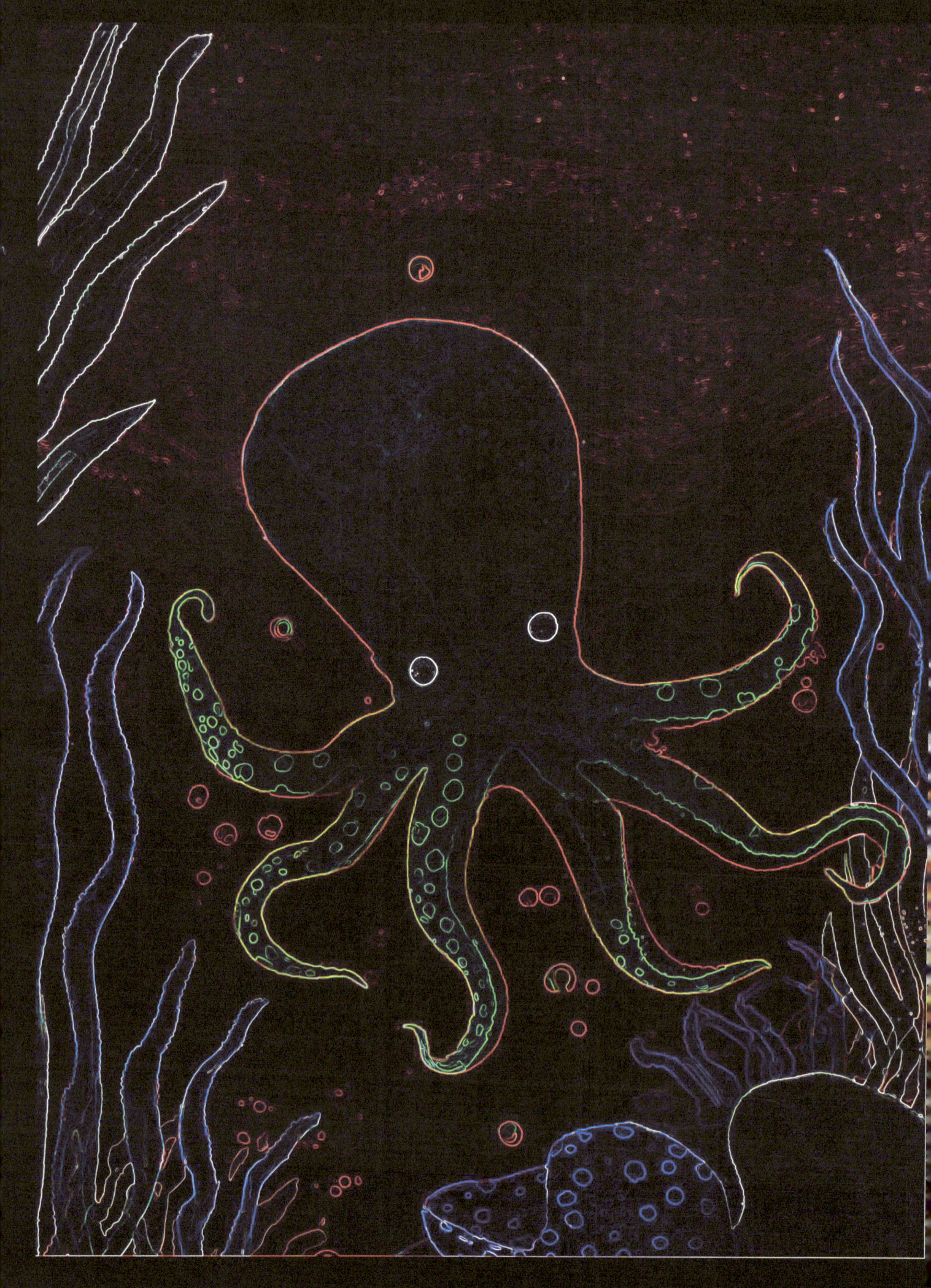

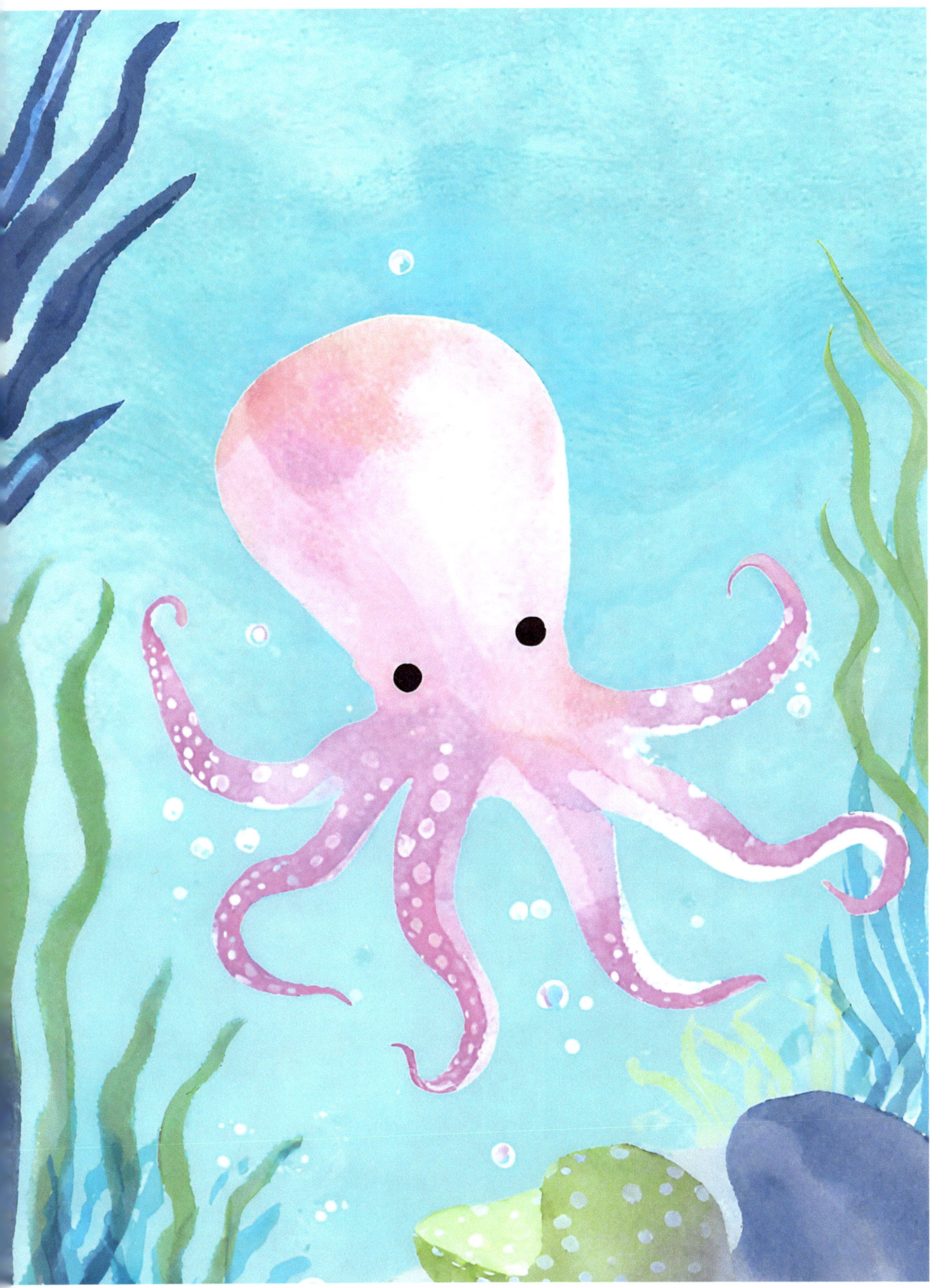

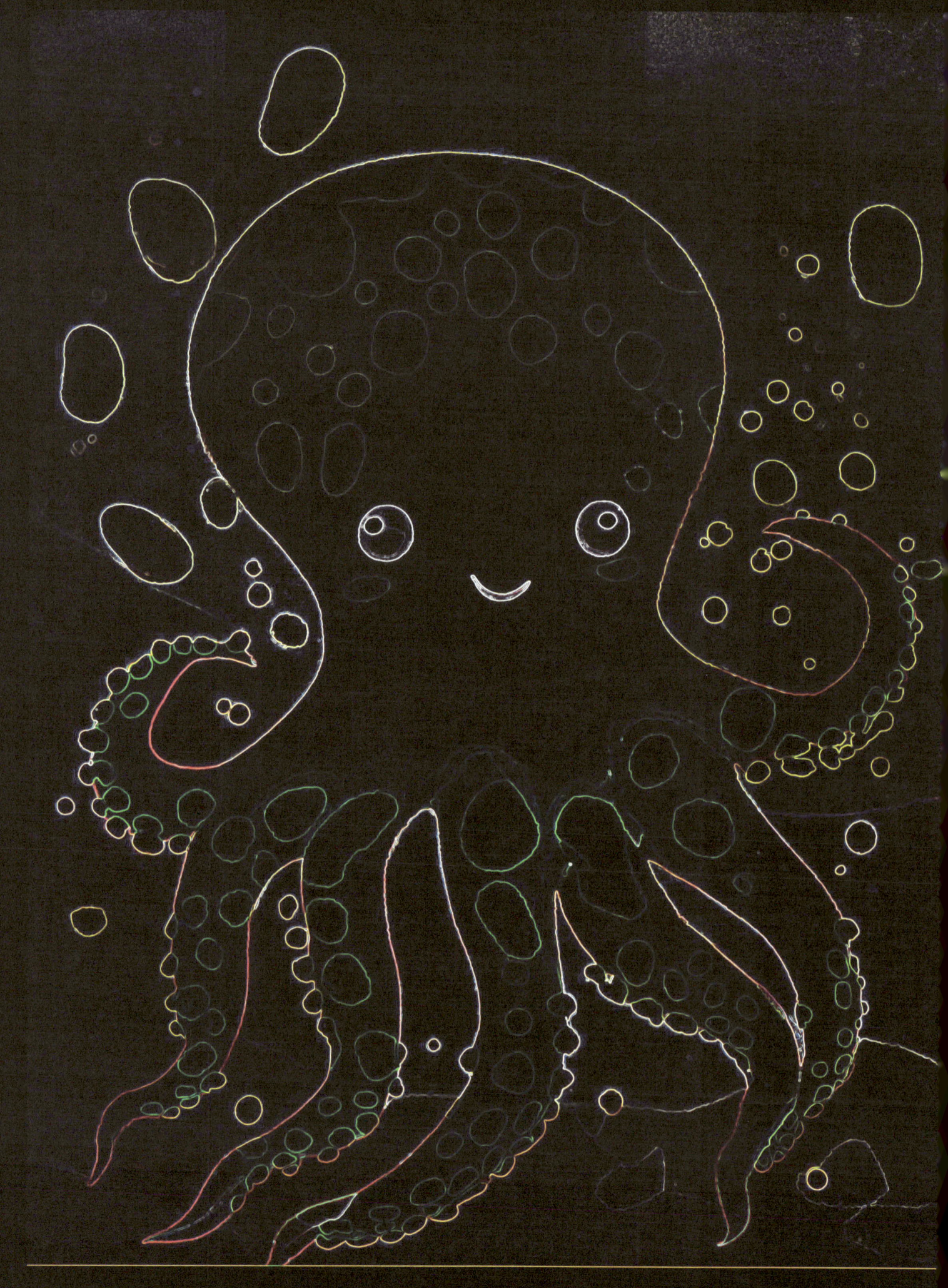

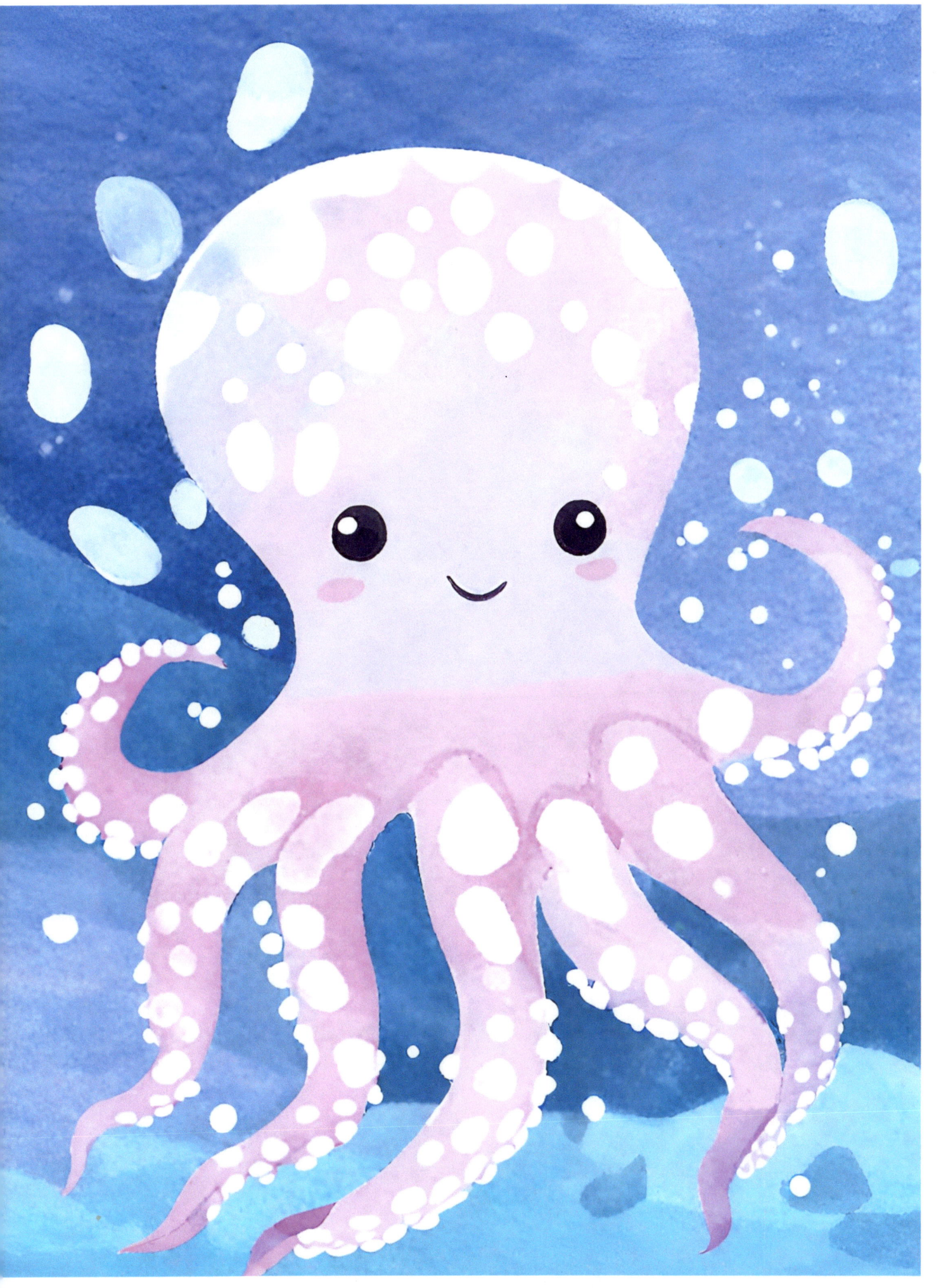

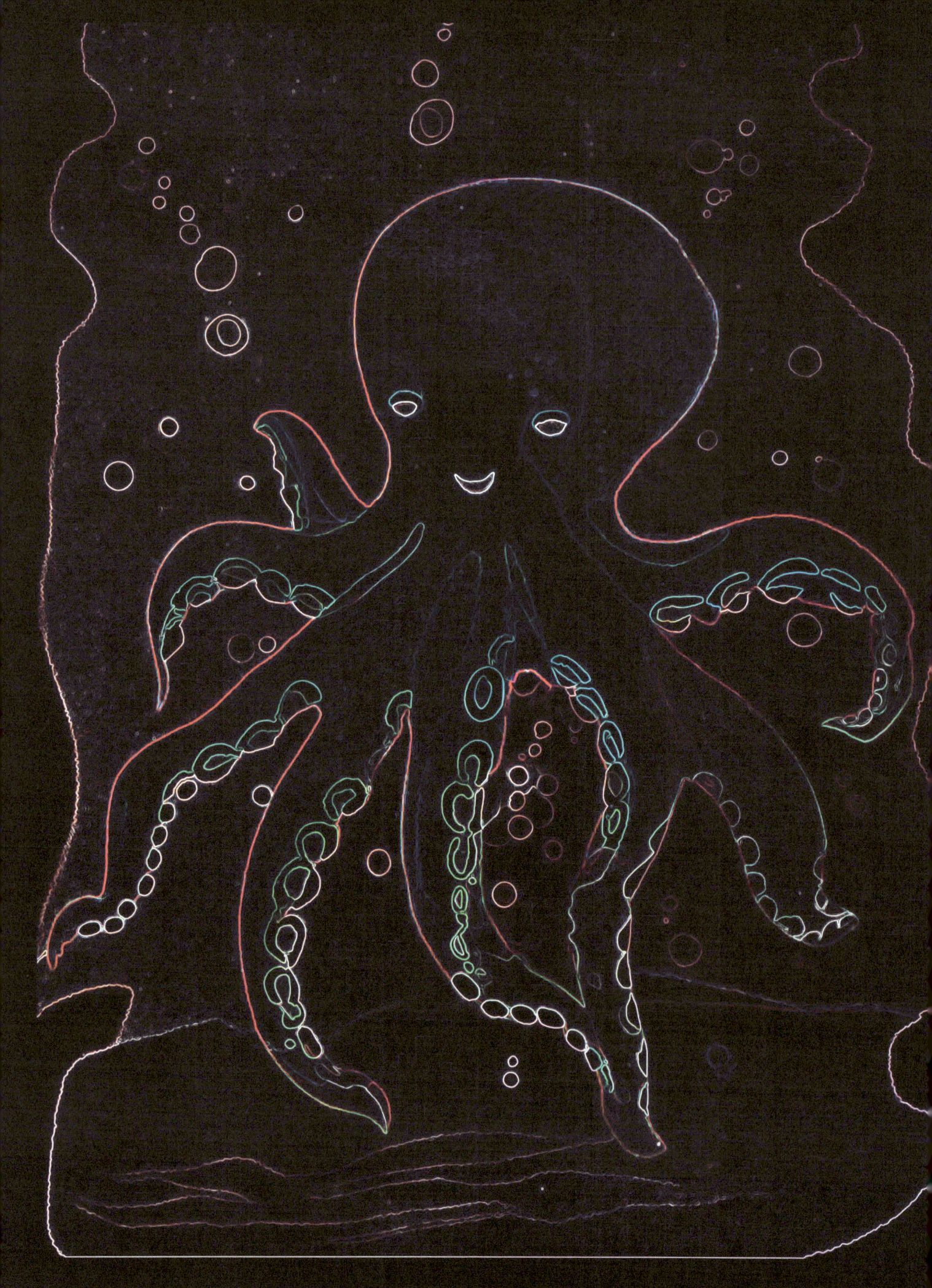

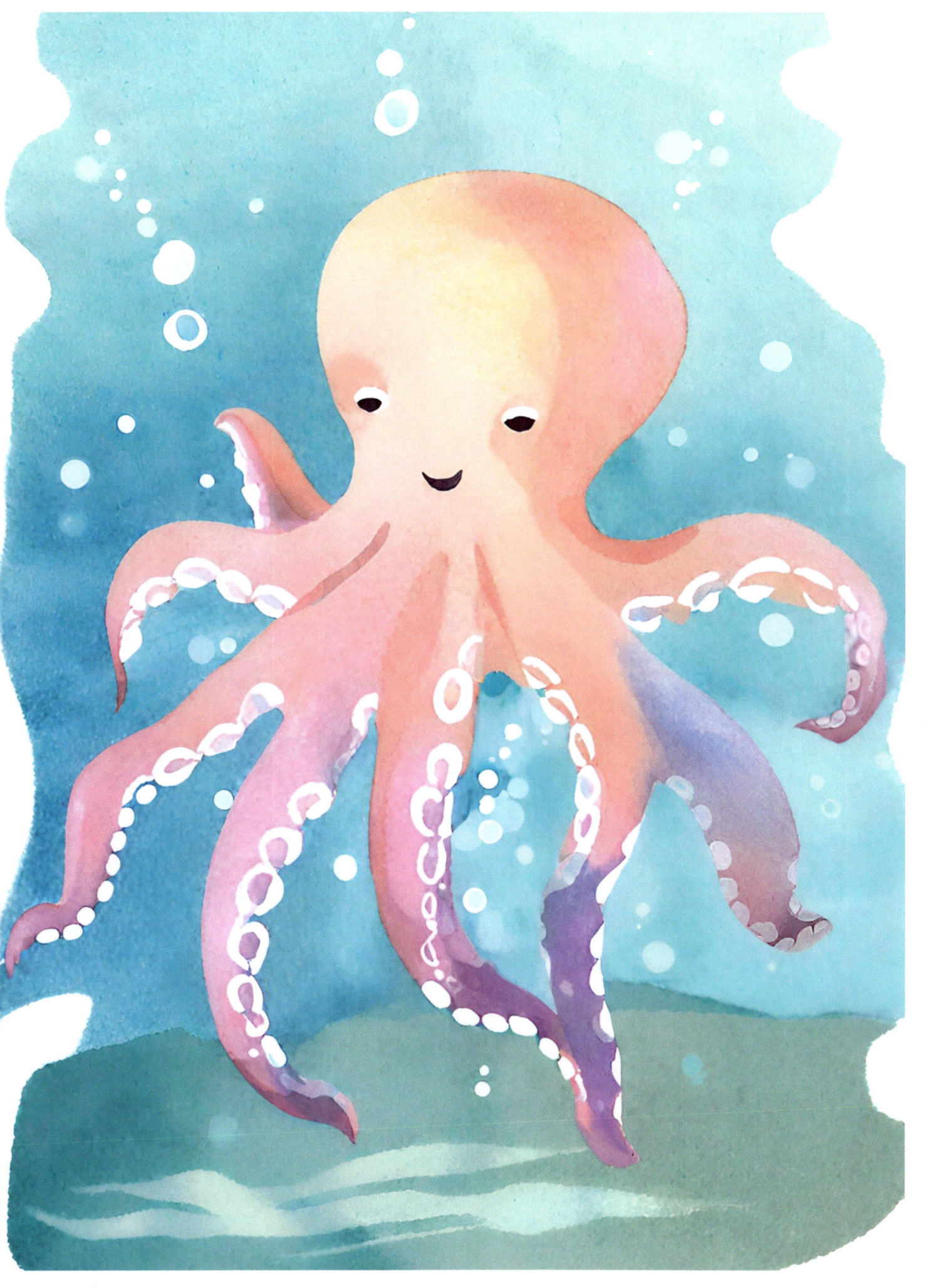

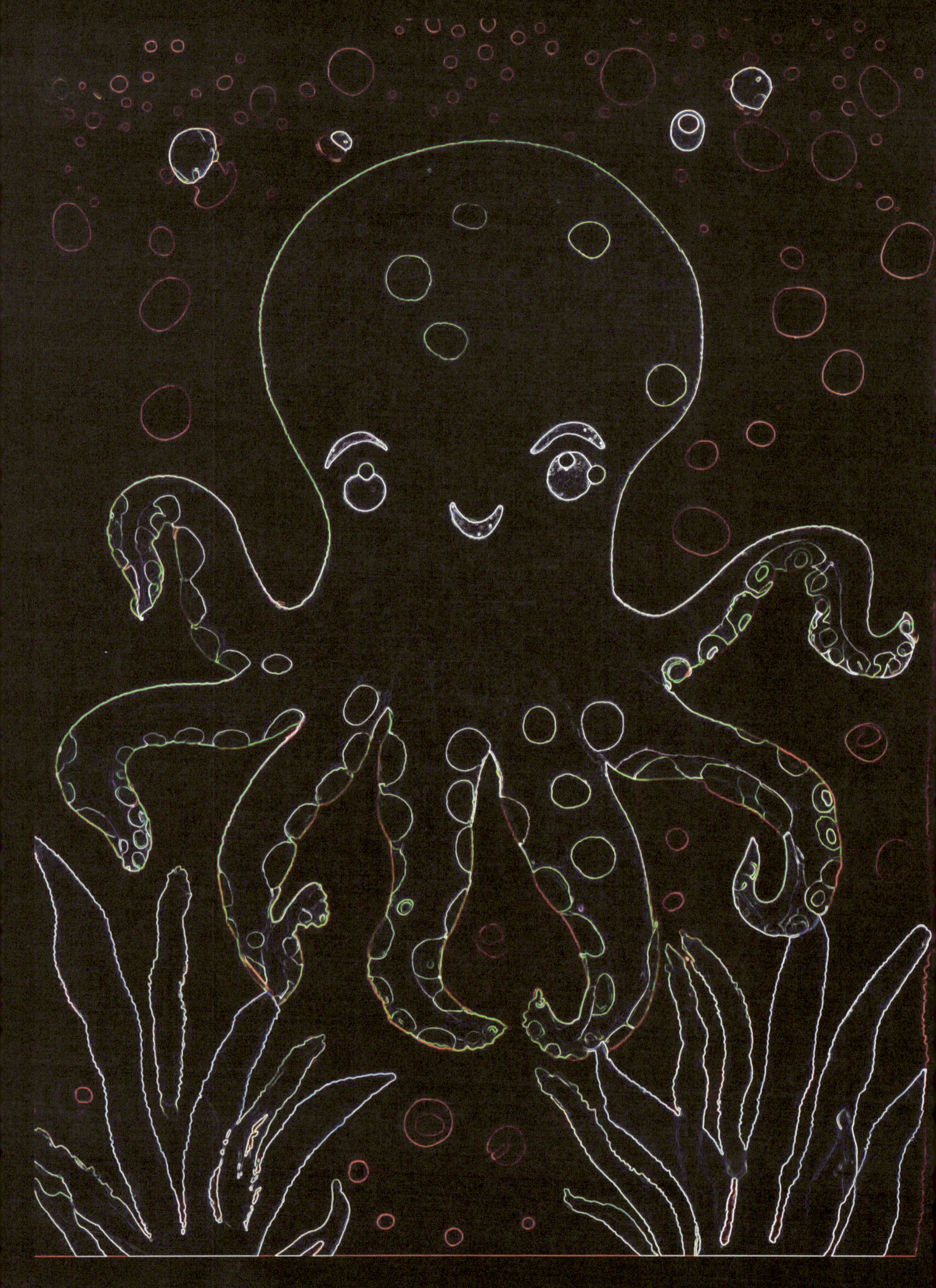

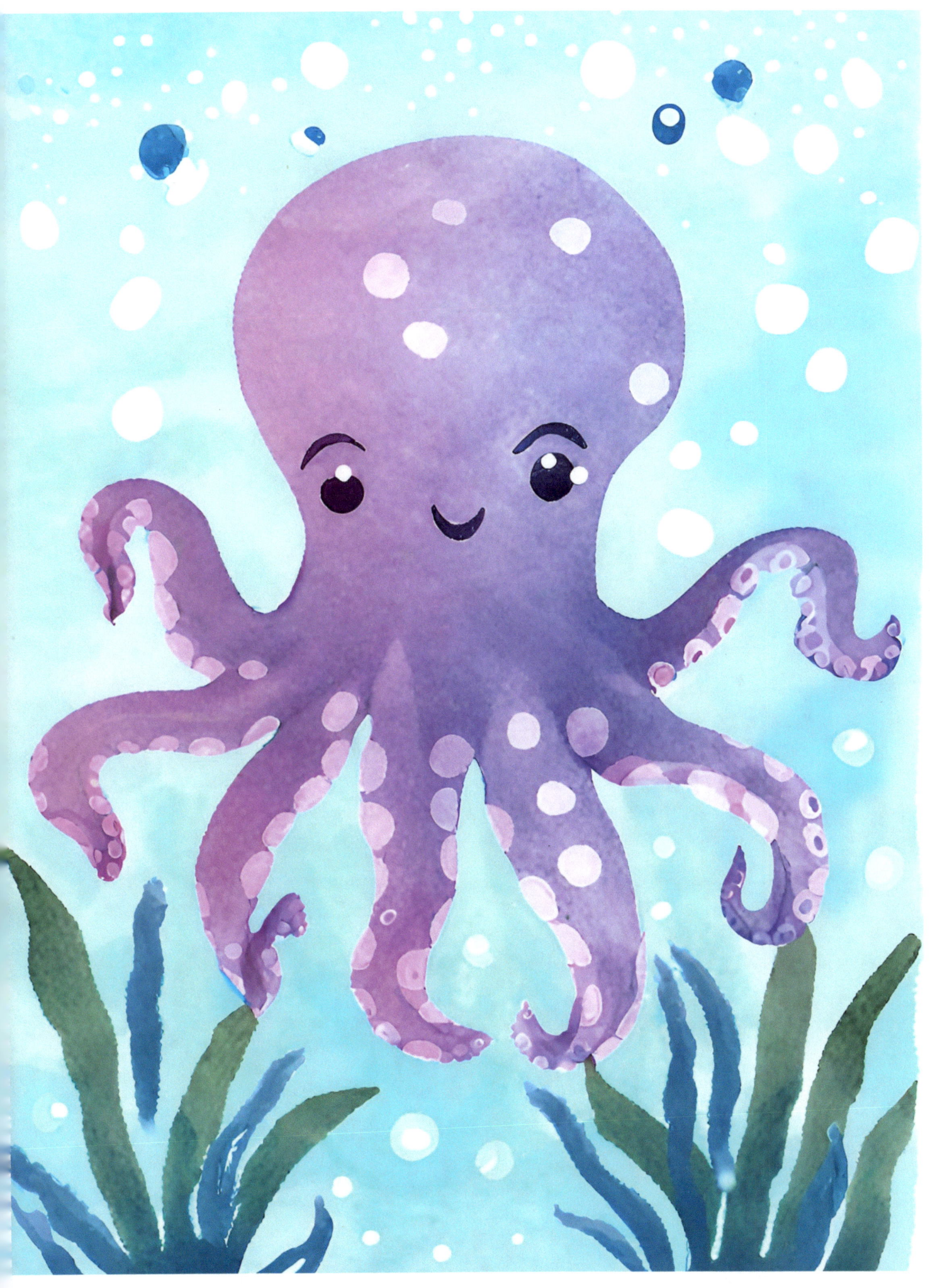

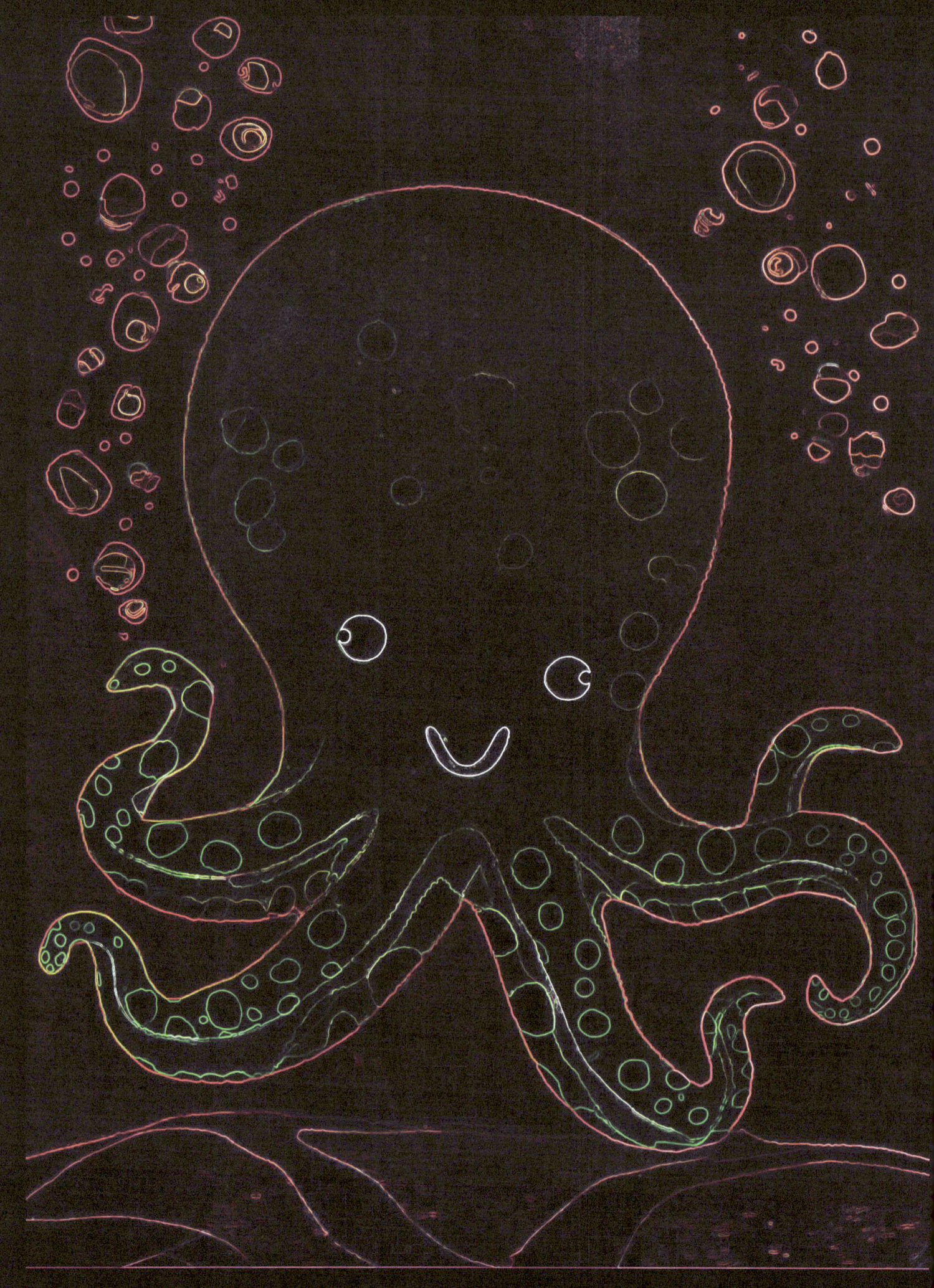

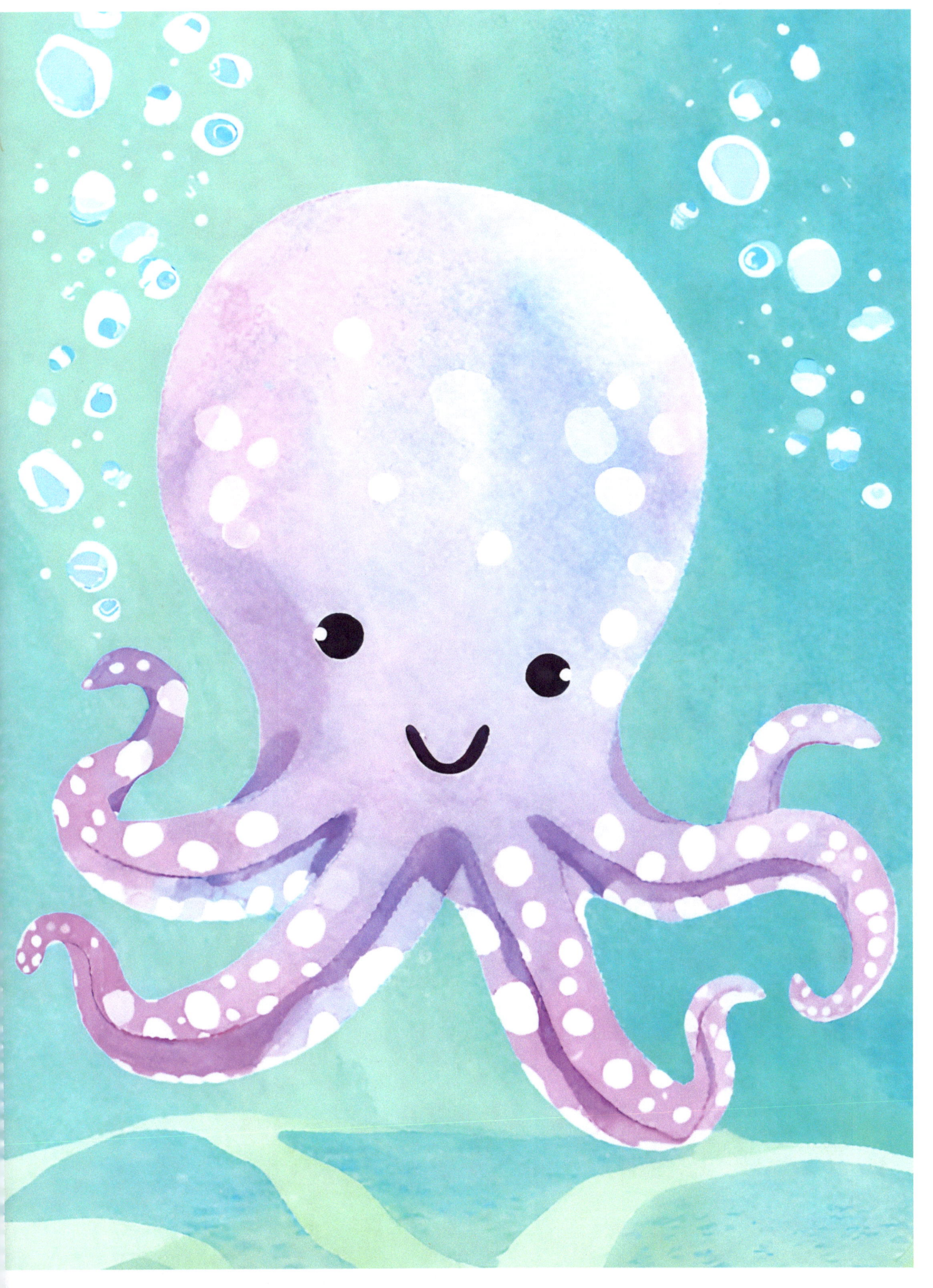

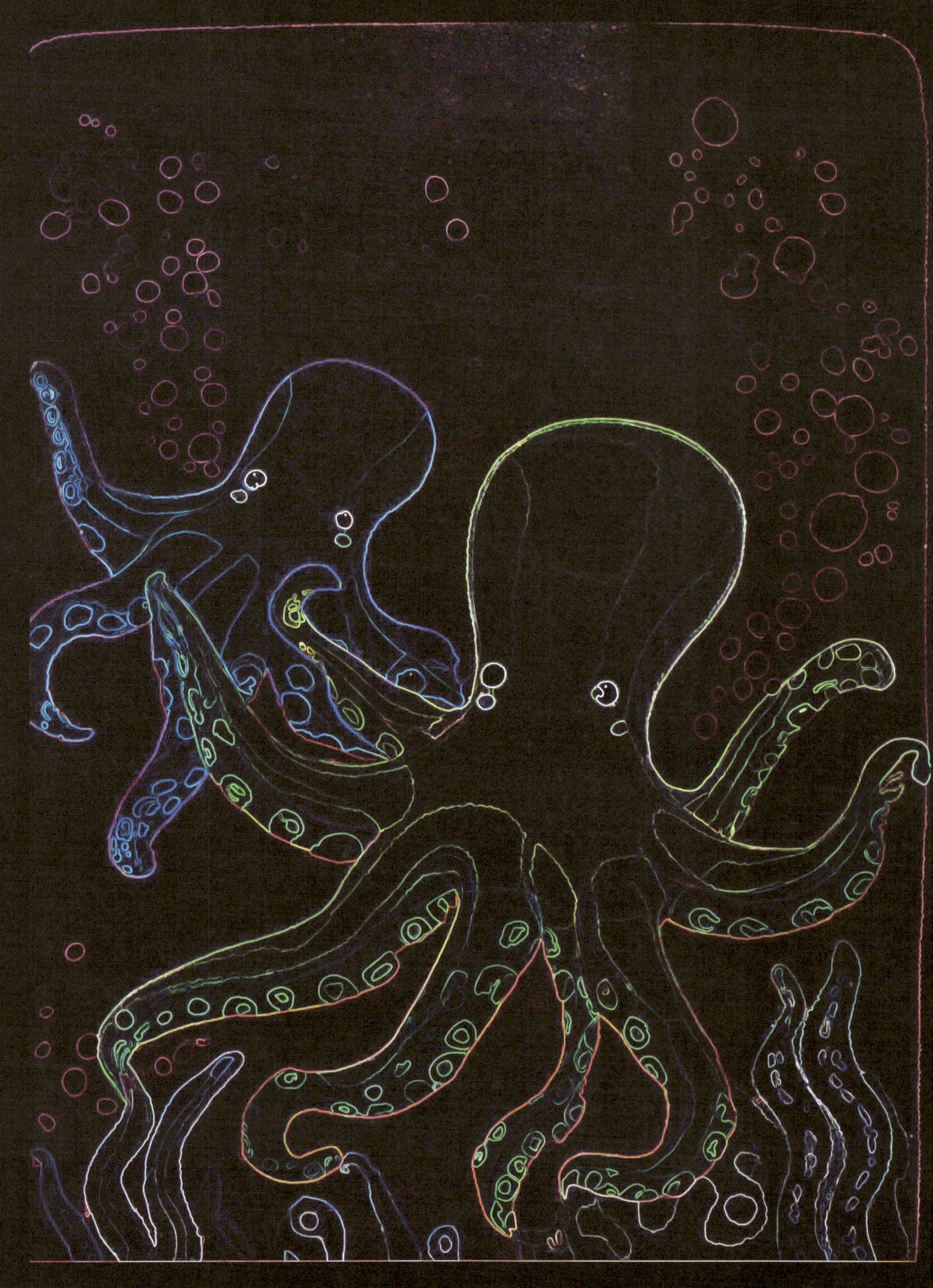

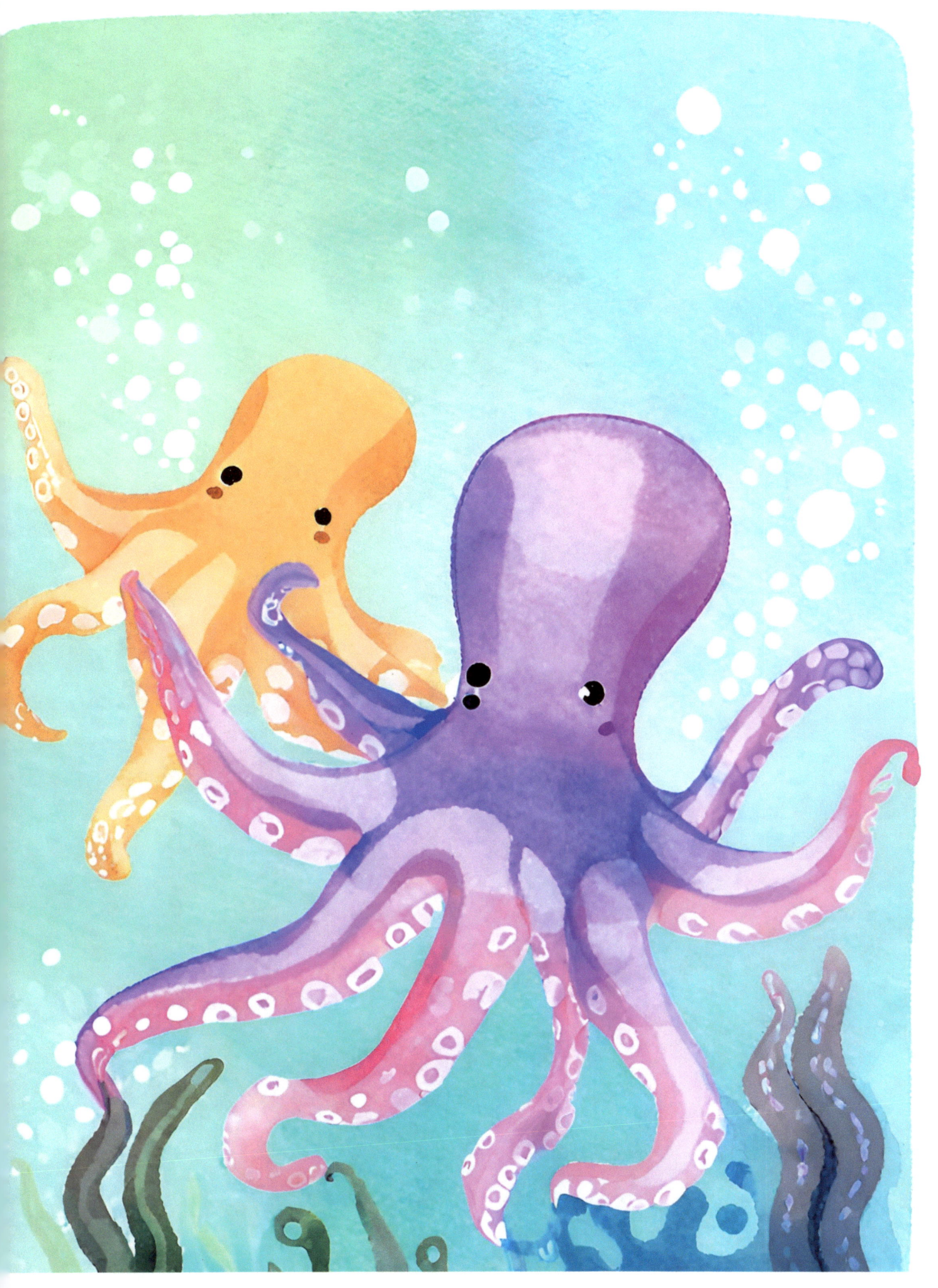

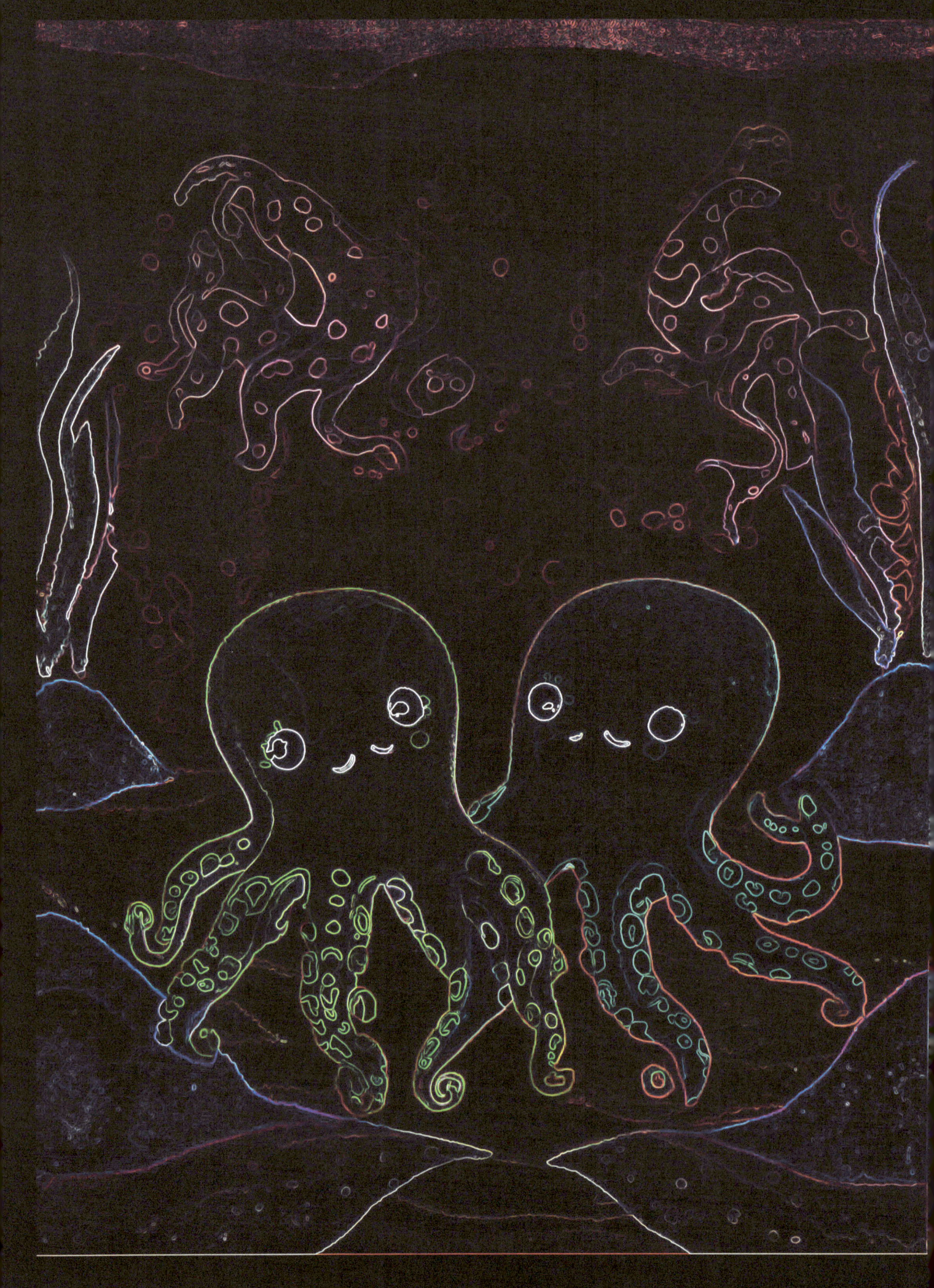

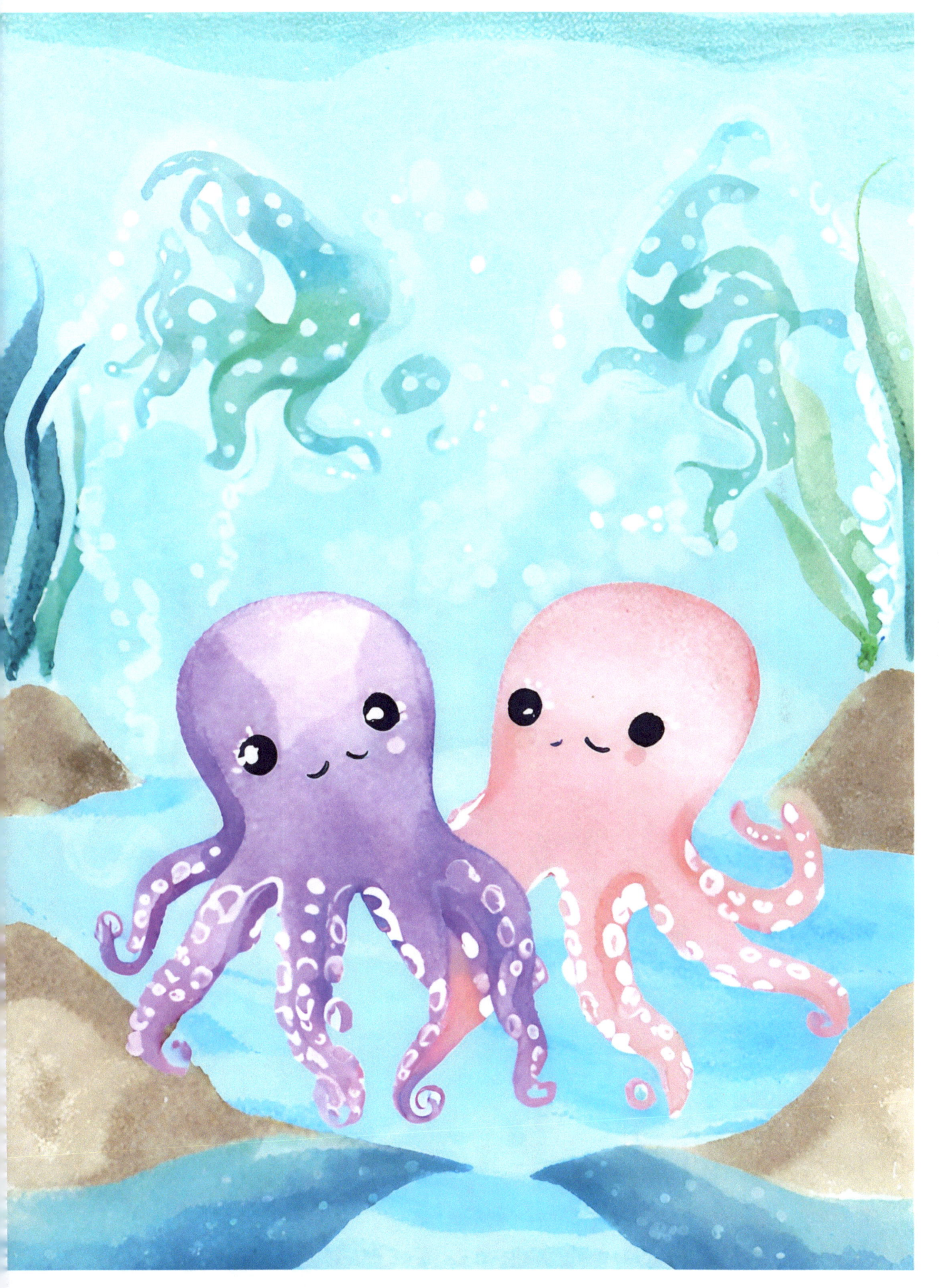

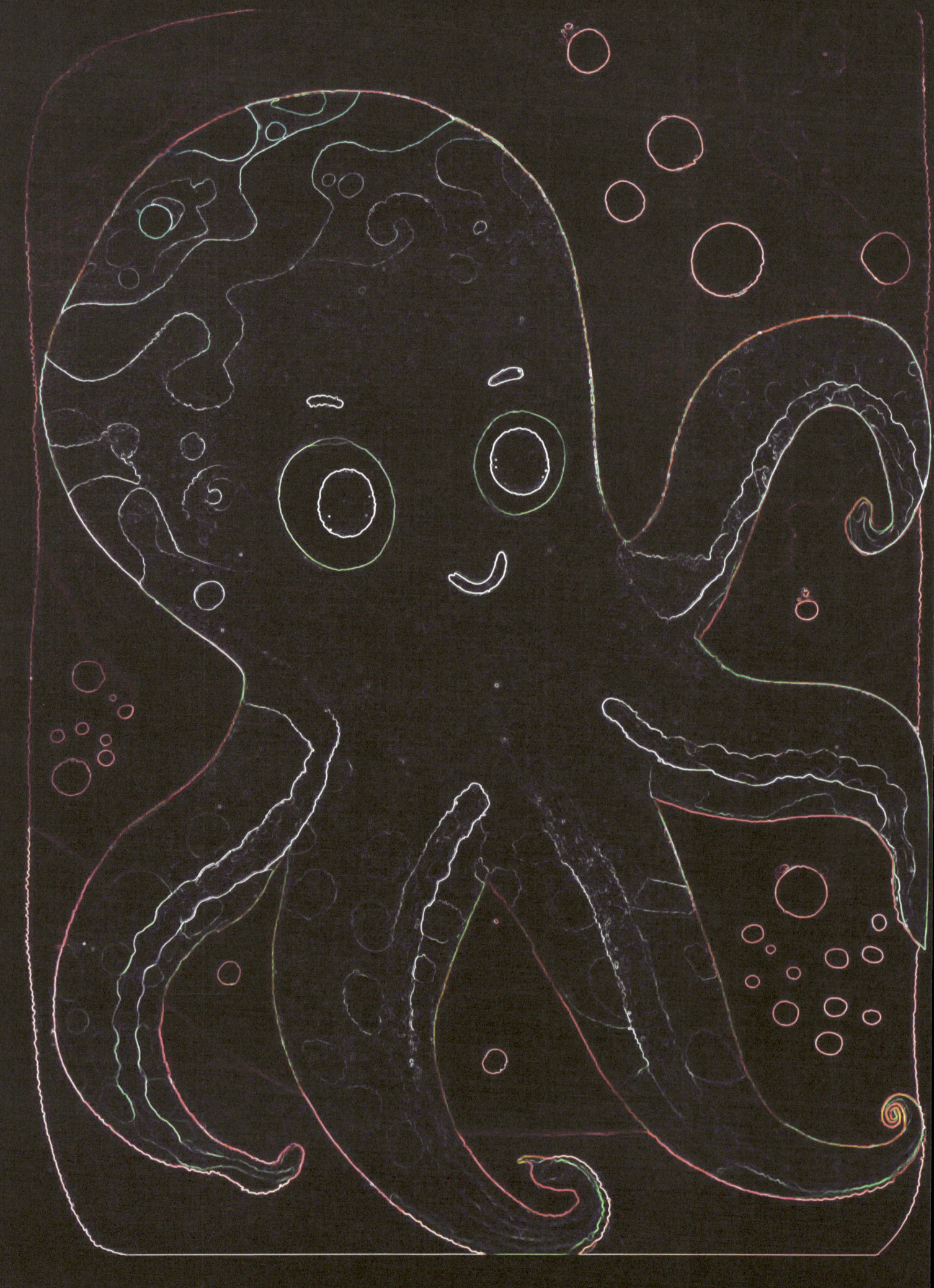

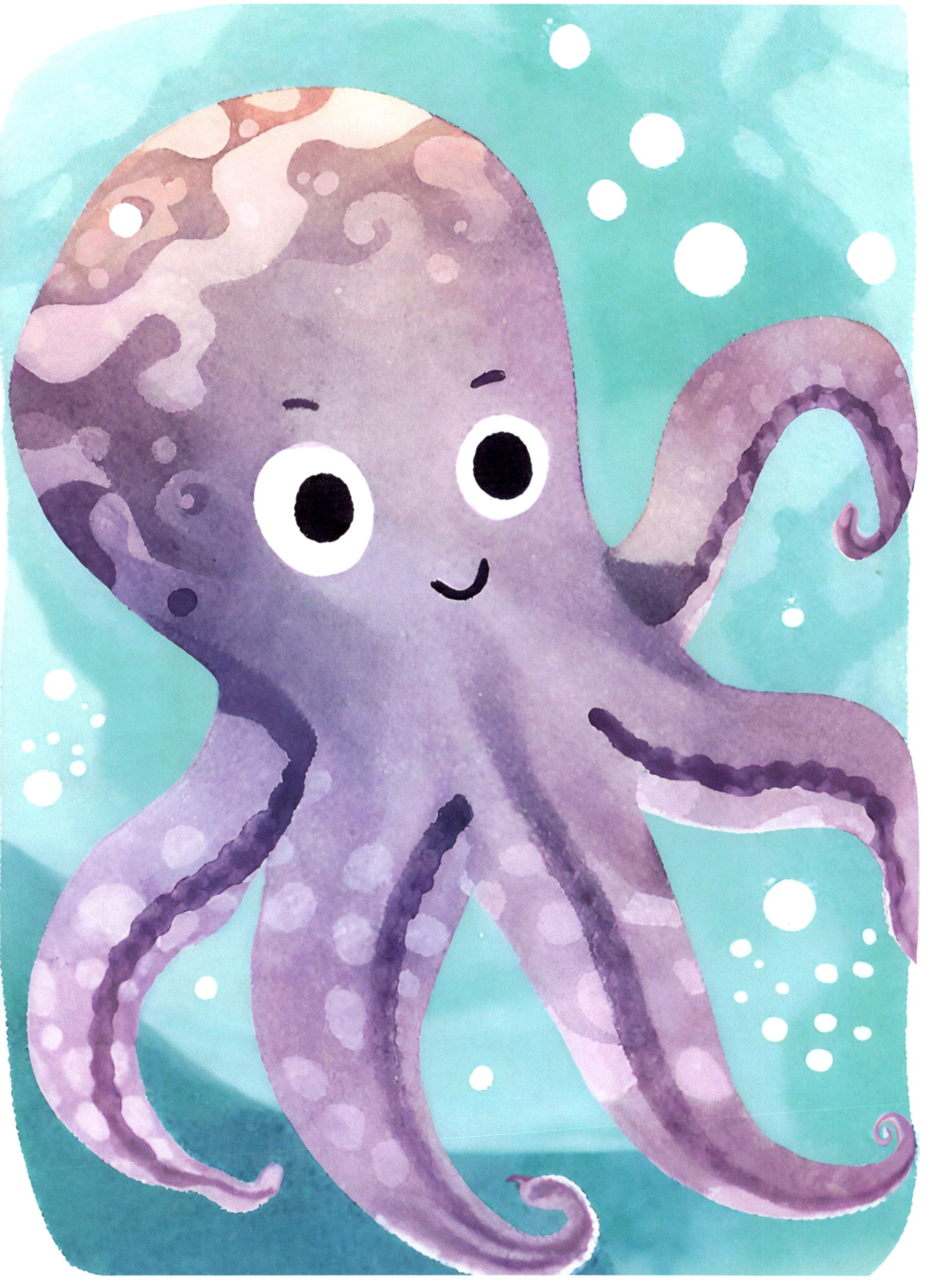

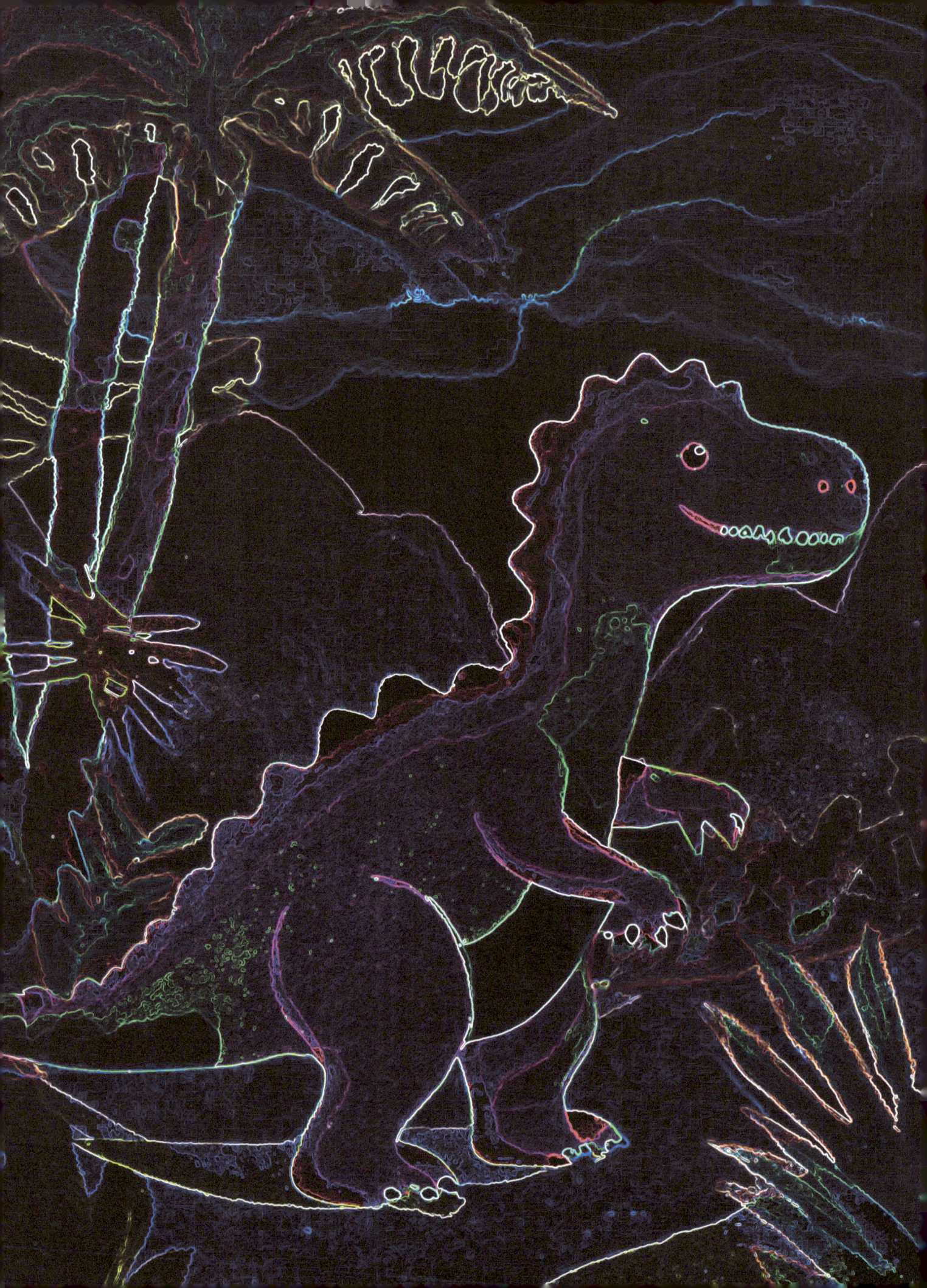

Thank You for buying this Octopus Reverse Coloring Book
SEE THE NEXT EDITION

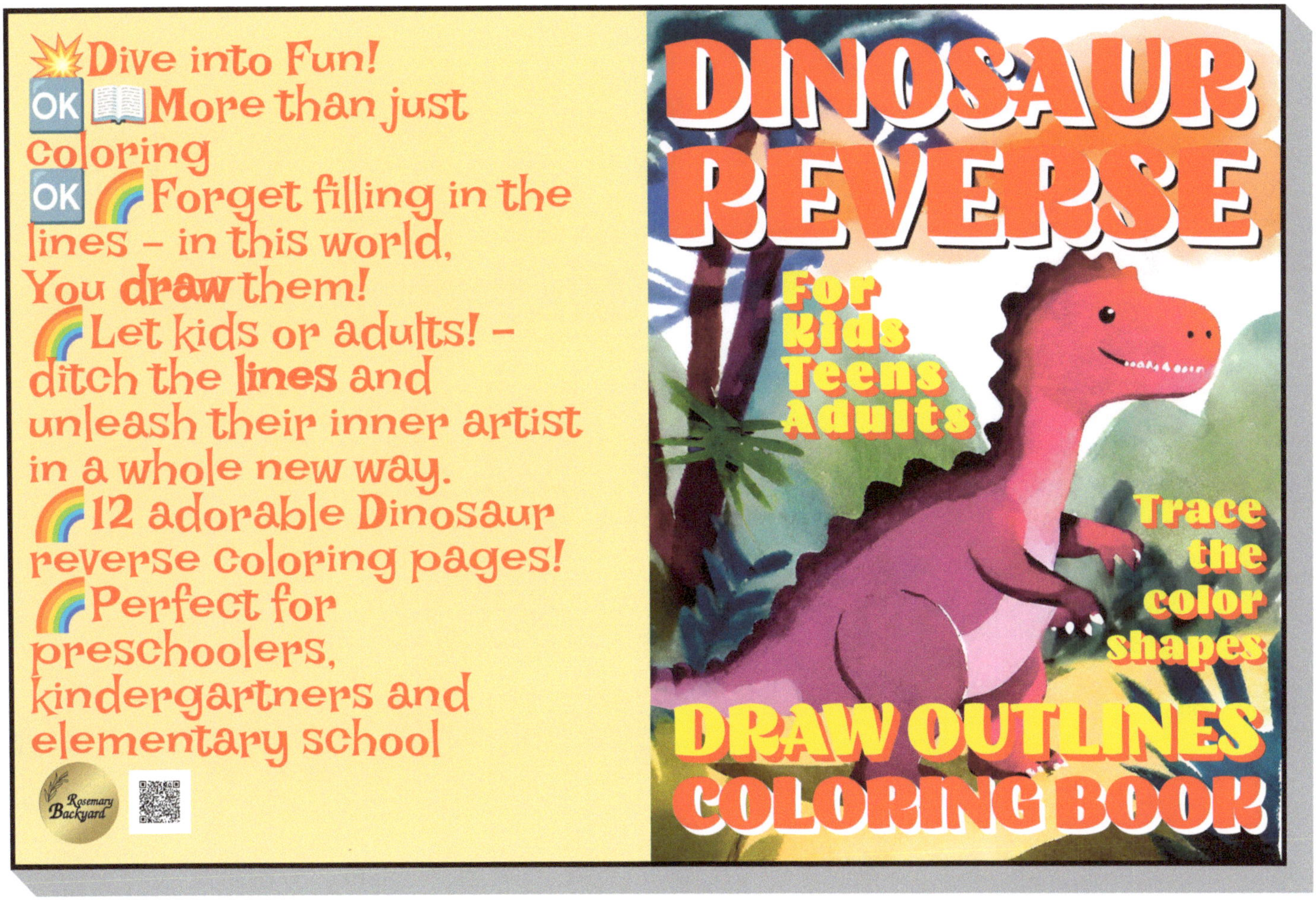

💥Dive into Fun!
🆗📖More than just Coloring
🆗🌈Forget filling in the lines – in this world, You **draw** them!
🌈Let kids or adults! – ditch the **lines** and unleash their inner artist in a whole new way.
🌈12 adorable Dinosaur reverse Coloring pages!
🌈Perfect for preschoolers, kindergartners and elementary school

DINOSAUR REVERSE
For Kids Teens Adults
Trace the color shapes
DRAW OUTLINES COLORING BOOK

Rosemary Backyard

Please leave a review

www.ingramcontent.com/pod-product-compliance
Lightning Source LLC
Chambersburg PA
CBHW041830280526
45792CB00006B/2039